30 Days of Me Devotional Journal

A Kickstart to Your Inner Healing Journey

La Ammitai

The Soul Blueprint

Edited by: Naleighna Kai www.naleighnakai.com
Cover designed by: J.L. Woodson www.woodsoncreativestudio.com
www.authorlaammitai.com

This publication is designed to provide general information regarding the subject matter covered according to science and personal experience. However, laws and practices often vary from state to state and are subject to change. Because each personal situation is different, specific advice given in this book should be tailored to suit the reader's particular circumstance(s). It is recommended that the reader consult with their primary advisors before engaging in the suggested activities of this book.

The author has taken reasonable precautions in the preparation of this book and believes the content presented in the book are accurate as of the date it was written. However, neither the author nor publisher assume any responsibility for any errors or omissions. The author and publisher disclaim any liabilities resulting from the use of the information contained in this book.

Words of Praise for *30 Days of Me*

"Have you ever read a book that changes your life day by day? Well I have. 30 Days of Me by La Ammitai is one such book. This journal / devotional is designed to make the reader take a journey into themselves to do the kind of self care and reflection that leads to lasting positive healing results. I whole-heartedly recommend this phenomenal book to anyone seeking the find their true selves and step into their purpose. Excellent resource. . I look forward to more amazing work from this gifted new author. — Stephanie M Freeman. #1 Bestselling Author of Survivor Stumbling Blocks to Stepping Stones.

"If you're ready to reclaim your authentic self; to be less exhausted with excess baggage; to breathe freely and thrive not just exist, then 30 Days of Me is for you. Thank you La Ammitai. This book and journal is what's needed to guide women on our journey to regaining our purpose and worth." - Patty Harris, #1 Bestselling Author of Comforting Those Who Grieve

"30 Days of Me is a literary masterpiece that will motivate you to reflect and become more self-aware of what changes you may want to make in your life. It will challenge you to identify things that may have been causing you to self-sabotage, deal with untapped emotions, and shed yourself of hinderances. I would highly recommend this book! — U.M. Hiram, #1 Bestselling Author of Persistence: The Power & Breakthrough of Fervent Prayers

"After participating in this 30-day challenge, I now know who the real Tiffany is — the true representation of the multifaceted intricacies of who I am. I have learned to embrace every part of me, which is the absolute best!"— Tiffany Hatchett

"This breathtaking journey helped me to break down my barriers, bring out my inner child, and be more patient and kind to myself. I am more positive and eager to go though each day with my head held high. I am unstoppable!"—Lakesha Taylor

"I no longer feel like I'm broken and unable to be fixed. I can feel myself healing and loving myself like I never have before. This is everything I need! Thank you La Ammitai for this experience. I am forever grateful for you."—Alisa Shaw

This 30-day journey came at a time when I felt lost and alone. The topics discussed, suggested activities, and journal assignments awakened my spirit.—Robrette McRae

"This 30-day journey was everything that I needed. It allowed me to explore things within myself in while diving deep within different levels and variations of shadow work."— Tiffani Didley

Dedication

I dedicate this book in loving memory of my:

Son, Kylon Greenwood
(July 2009 – Dec. 2009)

Father, William L. Greenwood Jr.
(Sept. 1965 – July 2018)

You are my greatest inspiration to live life intentionally and purposefully.
I will always love you.

Acknowledgments

I'm excited and grateful to enter the world of authorship. I'm equally appreciative for the love and encouragement from friends, family members, the original 30 Days of Me participants, and members of NK Tribe Called Success – a collective of bestselling authors. Thank you all for your unwavering support.

I give flowers to my mother, Jacquelyn Greenwood. Thank you for always believing in me even when it was nearly impossible to see my way through tough life challenges. You've been a soft cushion in circumstances where I fell hard. I'm grateful for the time, energy, resources, and wisdom you selflessly gift me. You are — and will forever be — my rock. I love you.

I give flowers to my grandparents, Dorothy and Leevell Eison. You two are the epitome of unconditional love. The greatest lesson I've learned from you is to always do what I love. I'm grateful for the weekends you keep my children, affording me time and space to self-care and/or have quiet time to work on my creative projects. Thank you for always rooting for my success.

I give flowers to my siblings, Zachary, Corey, Jaslyn, and Amari. You all play a significant role in my life journey in your own unique ways. One thing you all have in common is a great sense of humor. Humor fosters resilience. That's what you all have instilled in me. You bring good times and light-heartedness to my life. I love our tight-knit bond and wouldn't trade it for the world.

I give flowers to my children, Cameron and D'Angelo. Some of my greatest life lessons have been learned as your mother. I discovered my life purpose through you. You inspire me to live a life of devotion. I encourage you to dream big and fill your days with everything you're passionate about. Always know that I'm here to support you and be your biggest cheerleader.

I give flowers to my special friends, JCole, Brandon, and Morticia. Thank you for seeing and accepting me as I am, while also holding me accountable to continuous growth. You help keep me balanced and grounded through trials and tribulations. I appreciate our judgment-free chats on the phone and in person: brainstorming, venting, and sometimes just small-talking. I value our friendship and look forward to many more years together.

I give flowers to the 30 Days of Me course participants, Tiffany, Lakesha, Alisa, Robrette, Tiffani, Ednetra, Lakeysha, Ella, Alexis, Lenae, and Ja'Tavia. This book is a product of the 30-day healing journey we embarked upon in year 2020. You ladies are truly amazing. I'm extremely grateful and proud of every last one of you for seeing it all the way through with me.

I give flowers to NK Tribe Called Success leader, Naleighna Kai, and members, Stephanie M. Freeman, U.M. Hiram, Silk Wilson, and Patty Harris. I am grateful for the countless hours you spent with me on Zoom to help me cross the finish line. Thank you for taking the time to lay eyes on my work and offer your professional feedback. Your dedication to make sure no tribe member is left behind doesn't go unnoticed.

Last — but definitely not least — I give flowers to all of the NK Tribe members, my extended family, friends, and supporters. Thank you for showering me with positive energy, holding me accountable to complete my writing task, pushing me to reach my goals, and supporting me every step of the way. I'm forever grateful for you and consider every last one of you family.

Introduction

Commencement of the Journey

30 Days of Me started as a virtual self-development bootcamp in November 2020. We were in the dawn of the global Covid-19 pandemic. Many were infected and thousands of lives were lost. Fear, pain, and agony were displayed across all media outlets. My heart was heavy, my mind was clouded, and my emotions were a scattered.

Covid-19 was easily transmitted from one person to the next and was spreading at rapid speed. I often wondered if this was the end of time on earth for all. And if that were true, I knew it was imperative that I center and ground myself. I didn't want to transition from this life with any lingering pain, trauma, or should have-would have-could have's. It was time for a serious deep dive in shadow work.

Just like every other personal growth venture I embark on, my spirit advised me not to go it alone. So before I unplugged from social media and the rest of the world, I made a post inviting other women to join me on a 30-day hiatus.

In total, eleven women answered the call. Most of us were complete strangers to one another but that didn't stop us from being raw, real, and vulnerable right off the bat. Actually, it made it quite easier.

Wasting no time, we began promptly on November 1, 2020. Our intentions we set on self-discovery and recovery. We unpacked the heavy baggage we'd been carrying for days, months, and even years. We cried together, we laughed together, and we most definitely had fun getting to know one another. It was something about women showing up in their most authentic and genuine self that was remarkably beautiful and refreshing. We embraced the ugliest parts of ourselves — and each other — without shame, guilt, or judgment.

Some days were heavy and some were light. On the emotionally and mentally heavier days, we held time and space for one another to express and just be. On the lighter days, we indulged in various artsy activities to unleash our inner child — giving her permission to come out and play.

At end of our 30-day journey, we were met with a sense of relief, peace, and clarity. Even to this day, many of us keep in contact and check in from time to time. A true sisterhood bond was formed. For that, I'm forever grateful.

This process reminded of me the power and strength in numbers. Our vibe attracts our tribe. All we have to do is show up, step up, and speak out. We can go so much further and elevate even higher when we do it together.

It's All in the Numbers

The principles of the work in this book are primarily rooted in numerology. Numerology is the study of numbers and their deeper meanings/connections to life. In this book, you'll be working with the Pythagorean scale to include Cardinal Numbers 1-9 and Master Numbers 11, 22, and 33.

Each number has specific properties/energies associated with it. Recognizing them and flowing with them day-to-day will help you better understand yourself physically and spiritually. If you're dealing with a number greater than a Cardinal Number, but not a Master Number, reduce it by simply adding the digits together to get the collective energy. For example, take the number 12. To get the collective energy, find the sum of 1+2. 3. The number three harnesses the energies of creation, creativity, playfulness, youthfulness, joy, communication, and optimism. When you're dealing with the number three, these are the elements of focus.

Sound complex? Don't get discouraged. I break it all the down for you chapter-by-chapter, day-by-day.

The Best Version of Yourself Awaits You

Like many people, I struggled with the need for validation and people-pleasing. I was my own worst enemy. Unlearning that behavior was no easy task. However, it wasn't until I learned the importance and value of loving and caring for myself that I began to live a happier and freer existence.

Taking care of your own needs and not sacrificing them for the sake of someone else's is essential to your mental, emotional, physical, and spiritual well-being.

Gaining a high regard for your own needs, desires, and happiness will put you in a profound position to set better boundaries, unlock to your inner passions and gifts, and pour your life's devotion into this world.

Enter into a state of appreciation for yourself with this inspirational, transformational self-help book. When you best serve yourself first, you can then best serve others. You are who you've been waiting for. Welcome to 30 days of you with *30 Days of Me*.

La Ammitai

Day 1

1 (one)

Independence, individuality, self, leadership, action, innovation, originality, and new beginnings

Affirmation of the Day:

I choose me. I Am not in competition with anyone except the person I was yesterday.

Theme Song:

"Frequency" by Jhene Aiko

All numbers belong to the Universe, same as everything else in and of this world. How you choose to respond to them and experience them is completely up to you.

One of the most important numbers in Numerology is the number one. Being the root of all opportunities within us and in our lives, it calls you to focus on self in order to achieve your physical and spiritual goals. Everything starts with you.

Self-reliance breeds the absence of interference. It's time to start a new phase in your life and accept all the changes that come along with it. You already know what you know. So, release your fear of the unknown and accept the invitation to walk the path of uncharted territory. You'll be surprised at what you can discover about yourself when you surrender to the process.

We are all here with, and for, a greater cause or purpose. Get inquisitive about yourself. Begin asking yourself questions and allow your inner voice to respond. Who am I? What am I? Why am I? Where can I be better? How can I step into who I am destined to become?

Attempt to incorporate 30 days of something else that will benefit your journey. Maybe try 30 days of exercise, 30 days of intermittent fasting, or 30 days of meditation. Consult with your primary care provider before starting any exercise or diet plan. The point is to come up with something else that will aid in catapulting you to your next level during your 30-day journey.

Journal Entry:

In order to invite newness into your life, you first must let the things and people that are no longer serving you die. Start your first journal entry with "I commit to 30 Days of Me. During this 30-day devotion to myself, I release…" Then, make a list of all the things and energies that have been weighing heavily on you. (i.e. fear of judgment, procrastination, need for validation).

Once your release list is complete, make another list to fill the void of what you just emptied. Begin with, "I reclaim my power. I invite back into my space…" (i.e., self-acceptance, progression, or self-confidence).

Day 2

2 (two)

Partnership, balance, peacemaking, collaboration, and reflection

Affirmation of the Day:

The Universe wants what's best for my life. I relinquish my need to be in control and choose to work in collaboration with it for my highest good.

Theme Song:

"Crown" by Femme It Forward, Sinead Harnett

In numerology, the number two is regulated by feminine energy. Feminine energy is nurturing, cooperative, and receptive. We've been taught from an early age that if we aren't moving, then we're stagnant. This is far from the truth. Rest and reflection are progression too. Besides, how will we know if we're going in the right direction if we're constantly running?

We are all co-creators of our lives. We possess the power to either adapt to or change our perception of any circumstance that we face.

Being in alignment with the Universe will put you in the very position needed to flow gracefully through your life. This allows you to experience life with a little stress and a lot more joy.

Take this day to listen to the thoughts that cross your mind in your moments of stillness. Check in with your emotional state. How are you feeling? Why are you feeling it? Does how you feel relate to not currently being as far as you think you should be in life? If so, ask yourself… what it is that you desire to create?

Are there things you've been putting off because you feel time-deficient or bankrupt? Are you currently doing what you love or are you settling and operating with a scarcity mindset? When you do what you love, time and resources will expand and conform to heart's desire. Believe in what you truly want and feed it positive energy. This raises your vibrational focus. Shift your mindset, focus on your goals, and take action. You will reap the benefits of fulfillment.

$$Vibrational\ focus + action = fulfillment.$$

Self-reflection allows you to be consciously aware of where you've been and where you are now. We are all interconnected. People who come into your life, whether for a season or a lifetime, are a direct reflection of who you are or a reflection of aspects of yourself that you've been repressing. The latter calls for accountability and healing.

When we operate in awareness, we see things within ourselves that we wouldn't readily notice otherwise. Recognize the mirror reflections of those closest to you. Take a look at your people connections, i.e., friendships, relationships, and family. Give yourself time to evaluate your past and present circumstances.

Activity:

Take out a piece of paper. At the bottom of the page, draw a figure to represent you and where you are right now. At the top of the page, draw or use words to represent where you desire to be. The distance between the two represents space and time. Fold the paper in half to allow the top and bottom to merge as one. Now, you and your desires occupy the same space. Set this paper aside in a safe place to use later for a vision board activity.

Journal Entry:

What's the recurring theme in your past connections and circumstances? How have they affected how you see yourself and the ability to achieve goals? Write two other positive perspectives or outcomes to take the place of your negative outlook.

Day 3

3 (three)

Creation, creativity, playfulness, youthfulness, joy, communication, and optimism

Affirmation of the Day:

I honor my truth and express it in the most authentic way.

Theme Song:

"Belief" (Affirmations for Confidence) by Zil

Finding your own voice is one of the best feelings in the world. Expressing it unapologetically is even greater. "Your voice" is not restricted to vocal expression. Explore creative outlets you feel most comfortable expressing the things you're passionate about.

In a lot of cases, self-expression is a major area of struggle for people. When moments come for us to speak our truth, we find it frightening. It's almost equivalent to climbing to the peak of a mountaintop. You may have thoughts like, "Why would I want to go all the way up there when I'm perfectly rooted and grounded —and safe— here on flat land?" That's our comfort zone speaking to us. Standing up for ourselves and speaking out against all the things, people, systematic organizations that were imposed upon us but don't really resonate with our essence feels like that uphill climb.

This mindset is rooted in our childhood teachings, whether directly taught or visually learned behavior. We've ignored what no longer sits right with us in our hearts and our spirit long enough. It's time to get uncomfortable with conformity and start getting settled into our own personal truth.

Finding my own voice took me a while … a long while. When I was born, my father was in the military. The earlier portion of my childhood was more of a nomadic lifestyle. We lived in a few different states countryside. We've even traveled and lived in international areas.

My life felt constantly on the go, which made it hard for me to make and keep friends. I didn't want to become too attached to people I knew were only temporary. Eventually, the time would come where I'd have to say goodbye.

From one place to the next, I adapted and mutated to fit into whatever new environment I was thrown into. With each setting, there was always a new set of rules and regulations to follow. Even as an adult, this was one of my challenges. My natural flow tends towards being a freethinker and free-spirited. I despise feeling controlled. I conformed anyway. I gave in to the standard systematic way of living, which choked the life out of what my soul truly yearned for.

Eventually, I did the work. Truth is, I'm still doing the work, and I'm okay with forever being a student of life and beyond. I'm in love with my voice now. It's big, loud, proud, and full of passion and inspiration. It challenges what's presented at face value. It's philosophical and poetic. And what it has yet to become, I'm elated to embrace.

You see, people and systems count on our silence to keep us contained in a box. Break free, own your energy, and co-create the life you desire. Ground yourself in all things that ignite your creative fire. Your truth will always fulfill and satisfy you. If you have to convince yourself of a belief, or if someone has to convince you, it doesn't belong to you. Give it back.

Journal Entry:

What are your beliefs about yourself? What are your beliefs about society? What are your spiritual beliefs? Write about them all and include your reasoning why. Consider what beliefs you hold on to that someone else gave to you. Do any of them not sit right with you? Record your thoughts and feelings.

Day 4

4 (four)

Foundation, structure, stability, building, discipline, and the body

Affirmation of the Day:

I love my body and I Am comfortable in my own skin.

Theme Song:

"444" by Gayathri Krishnan

Do you believe that maintaining your health simply means avoiding foods that are unhealthy? It's not enough to just avoid foods that are high in calories, sodium, and such. We must take a more active approach by adding daily habits to enrich our overall well-being.

Start the process of figuring out how to strengthen your discipline and motivation to take better care of you. Facilitate an inventory of the cravings and not-so-good habits you fall victim to. One habit to start with is your mindset. Do you feel time-poor when it comes to diet and exercise? Has the emphasis on physicality by societal standards caused you to stress out to the point of giving up? These types of things impact us but not in a good way. It causes us to become negatively obsessed with our bodies and our health.

It's highly important that we honor ourselves as spiritual beings having a human experience. And within this experience, the body is the temple in which the soul resides. Even though our bodies don't represent our true essence, there is a connection between our health and how/what we manifest into our reality. The goal is to manifest from our most spiritually present and vibrant selves. Once we recognize this connection and take affirmative action, we can then develop better habits, attitudes, and a healthier temple to enrich our experiences on our journey.

Activity:

Take out a piece of paper. At the bottom of the page, draw a figure to represent you and where you are right now. At the top of the page, draw or use words to represent where you desire to be. The distance between the two represents space and time. Fold the paper in half to allow the top and bottom to merge as one. Now, you and your desires occupy the same space. Set this paper aside in a safe place to use later for a vision board activity.

Journal Entry:

What's the recurring theme in your past connections and circumstances? How have they affected how you see yourself and the ability to achieve goals? Write two other positive perspectives or outcomes to take the place of your negative outlook.

Day 5

5 (five)

Change, challenge, risk, freedom, adventure, transition, and transformation

Affirmation of the Day:

I Am the author of my story. I give myself permission to change the narrative of old chapters and write new ones any time I choose.

Theme Song:

"Free" by Perri Jones

The only thing that is constant in and of this Universe is change. Everything and everybody changes. Which direction we decide to flow is left up to our own free will. In order to invite forward-motion transformation, we must first heal what's been holding us hostage for so long.

New opportunities are sometimes right in our face. We either don't recognize them or we feel we aren't ready for them. When spiritual transformation comes knocking at your door, it's not asking you to invite it in, it's commanding you to. When you shut the door on the opportunity presented to evolve, you only send yourself back through past cycles of hard lessons to learn — or in this case, re-learn.

Maybe you've been feeling stuck lately. Or maybe at every turn in your life there seems to be a conflict that arises and raw emotions begin to spill out. These are tell-tale signs that you are on the brink of a major shift in your life.

Does your relationship/marriage leave you feeling unsatisfied? Is your job unfulfilling? Are you having a difficult time communicating with your children? These types of moments and feelings often cause us to blame and judge others because we don't want to take responsibility and accountability for the role we play in our own discontent. We also sometimes develop a fear of losing what we've worked so hard to build,

Change and transformation is natural. Trust the process. If you are getting big signs from the Universe, pay attention and flow accordingly. You're being offered the answers and support you need in this moment to get you to where you ultimately desire to be. You get tested the most when it's time for you to elevate. Don't break.

Journal Entry:

Are you satisfied with your life right now? List 5 challenges you are facing right now. How are they holding you back from pursuing your passions? List 5 ways you can invite positive change to replace your challenges.

Day 6

6 (six)

Home, love, family, relationships, harmony, and humanity

Affirmation of the Day:

I value myself. I take personal time daily to self-care.

Theme Song:

"Scuse Me" by Lizzo

Self-love and care are the state of appreciation for yourself and having a high regard for your own well-being and happiness. Practicing it means to put your needs first and not repress them for the needs of others.

Spending some you-time is of utmost importance. No one can water your garden and tend to your weeds better than you. You can best serve yourself by:

- Talking to/about yourself with love

- Prioritize your needs and desires

- Accept yourself as you are right now

- Don't judge yourself too harshly

- Set healthy boundaries

- Fall in love with your authentic self

Also, pay attention to what you consume mentally and physically. Energy is everything, and everything is energy; Energy in is energy out. What you think and how you feel is what you come to experience. What's in motion intentionally becomes what you deem as your reality. So, be mindful of your thoughts, beliefs, and feelings toward yourself.

Activity:

Do something nice for yourself today. You deserve it. Maybe you can take a walk, have a spa day, buy something new, or just relax and read a book.

Journal Entry:

Write a love letter to yourself. Be sure to include your past, present, and future self. Forgive and make amends with who you used to be. Speak life into who you are now and who you are becoming. Make promises you intend to keep to yourself.

Sample:

A Love Letter To Myself – La Ammitai

Dear Me,

It's nice to finally know you. For so long, you were a stranger to me. I often wondered who you were, but I didn't have the courage to approach you. It was just so much easier to blend in and conform to everything and everyone else around me.

I've embodied multiple identities, mutating myself into what felt good in that moment. I should have sought you out, but I didn't. I always knew you were amazing, but I often doubted that I could show up for you daily. Instead, I chose lifestyles that neglected my higher-self simply because it was easier.

I allowed you to be manipulated, mentally and emotional abuse while you waited for me; dying for me to stand up for you. I allowed you to be judged and ridiculed. This caused you to be filled with hate, anger, resentment, bitterness, and shallowness.

When you couldn't bare anymore, I watched you disconnect from yourself and from the world. At that time, I felt helpless. I didn't know what to do.

I offer you my sincerest apologies for not fighting for you – for not believing in you and not being there for you. I apologize for not loving you the way you deserve to be loved.

I say to you now … no more! No more feeling awkward or out of place. No more feeling unworthy. You are valuable. You are limitless. No more feeling ashamed. I accept you for you. No more feeling like you aren't enough. You are and will forever be more than enough. You have every right to be all that you are — and in your image, you are beautiful.

I love you, unconditionally. I now put you first. You are my priority. I vow to never lose you again. Coming back from all of what you've been through showcases your resilience. I honor, value, and respect you for that. I promise that you'll never experience anything like it ever again.

I am here to protect you, love you, and care for you. I commit to nurturing you, healing you, and growing with you. I am here to provide you with everything, and I mean everything, that you need.

You deserve it.

Love,
Me

Day 7

7 (seven)

Self-discovery, solitude, knowledge, wisdom, truth, and the deeper meanings to life

Affirmation of the Day:

I know that I Am here for a purpose and I Am grateful for my journey.

Theme Song:

"Did It For Myself" by MLXVE

Every last one of us is here on this earth for a specific reason. We all possess innate talents, gifts, and skills to bring to the world. That is our purpose. When we walk in our vocation, we find it to be meaningful and satisfying work.

What you identify as your path may look a little different from others. That's okay. Your purpose is unique and can shift throughout life in response to your ever-changing and evolving circumstances and experiences.

Some people resist pursuing their life purpose because they feel like they do not have what it takes to show up as their highest self. Others may be stuck at identifying the natural gifts they possess and feel clueless about exploring them.

Your inquisitiveness about your life purpose may arise at any given time, and again, may change with each cycle of your life. In most cases, people start questioning the deeper meanings to their existence during times of transition, chaos, or crisis. Things like the loss of a job, loss of a loved one, or a terrible breakup are just a few examples of events that may signal you're on the verge of an awakening period. So yes, your special gifts that set you apart from others are one part of your truth. The other half is your connection to people and things. This is why crisis is a common symptom of isolation-transformation.

It's important that you remain mindful in your times of solitude, especially following a traumatic experience, to ensure you don't fall victim to depression and anxiety. Instead, utilize your moments of stillness to open your mind and heart to what the Universe is communicating to you and through you in the midst of your circumstances. Take some time to read, study something new, write, or indulge in some art therapy. These are all valuable reflective processes to guide you towards clarity and understanding.

Journal Entry:

Living a happy life is individualistic. Living a purposeful life is universal. If money or responsibilities weren't a factor, what would your life look like? How can you make that life your reality?

Day 8

8 (eight)

Power, authority, abundance, prosperity, wealth, and business

Affirmation of the Day:

I have everything I need to be successful.

Theme Song:

"Proud of You" by Kalieha

We've all heard the phrase, "You are your own worst enemy". This holds true if you're one of many who are stuck in a scarcity mindset. Operating in your survival mode and playing small makes it harder to go after what you really want in life.

Do you deal with patterns of negative self-talk like, "I'm just not good enough" or "This is too hard, I can't do it?" Are you worried about how you will be received by others if you follow your heart and dreams? These are the exact types of thoughts that hold you back from showing up and actually achieving your goals. Transform your thoughts and feelings of lack into a positive, abundant mindset.

An abundance block is a mindset block. One of the worst things you can do is not fulfill your dreams, desires, and goals, especially when the reasoning is centered around what other people think about your journey. At the end of the day it's your journey not theirs. The vision of your life destiny was given to you and only you. It needs no validation from outside sources.

An abundance mindset means to recognize the boundless potential in your life and everything around you. As a result of seeing it, you start believing it. That alone gives you the drive and determination to create the life your heart desires.

Think big, be big, and do big things. Operate day-to-day with a growth mindset. Believe that there's always room to improve and be better than you were yesterday. See your glass as half-full instead of half empty and there's more than enough around you to fill your cup. Perspective is golden.

With an abundance mindset, you feel free and find joy in sharing and giving to others. Truth be told, giving is one of the quickest ways to receive. First, cultivate the energy you wish to receive. Then, give it away. By giving freely, you set the intention that there is more where that came from. It'll come back to you tenfold. Today, give some of your time, energy, resources, or money to someone in need.

Journal Entry:

Gratitude is the attitude. When you express thanks to the Universe for the things you have and for what's actually working in your favor, you set yourself up to receive more of the same type of energy.

Write about all the things, people, and circumstances you're grateful for. Go into detail about how they've made such a positive impact on your life.

Day 9

9 (nine)

Cycle completion, endings, release, compassion, inspiration, and enlightenment

Affirmation of the Day:

I let go of past regrets and express gratitude for the lessons my past missteps have taught me.

Theme Song:

"Bravo" by Ledisi

Reflect on the past eight days. You've come this distance. Now, let's start weeding the garden and counting the wins — big and small. Take an inventory of yourself and your current environment. Since you've started this 30-day journey, what or who in your life is no longer in alignment with where you see yourself heading? Cut the cord!

Sometimes we allow things and people to hold space and overstay their welcome in our lives out of a sense of loyalty or obligation. We even sometimes feel like we have the courage to let them go only when something goes wrong, like a big argument with a loved one or a demotion on the job. But what would it look and feel like if we could just let go with love and peace? What if we simply show respect for the energy, acknowledge what it came to teach, and then send it back to the Universe to prepare for our next cycle?

All things have an expiration date. Death is a natural part of life. The word death is not subjective to physical form; it is also metaphorical. Death and I have an interesting relationship and an understanding. From my own perspective, nothing is ever lost or a loss —even in death. It simply evolves. When things come to an end, I can allow my emotions to swallow me in a black hole and stay there or I can use the knowledge and wisdom the experience afforded me to elevate higher. I'll take the latter.

I personally practice logic over emotion. My feelings are still very real and valid. I choose to be a reflective being, constantly questioning why, with the intent to learn and elevate. This is where I experience most of my greatest epiphanies and solutions to any given situation.

In this period of cord-cutting, let go with love and thanks. Acknowledge all the goodness that's still present in your life, whether tangible or intangible. Make room in your vessel and environment for a brighter new start. Something great is getting ready to be birthed proceeding this period of death. After every ending, there's a new beginning. You just have to send it an invitation.

Letting go doesn't mean forgetting. In the context of this chapter, it means to process past and present events while recognizing:

- Any open, unhealed wounds
- What no longer resonates with where you are now and where you're going
- When to cut the cord and move forward with peace

In your journal, number your page 1-9. Now take some time to evaluate nine things/people in your life today. Start each with, "Does this [insert thing/person] serve me anymore?" If your answer is yes, write how so. If your answer is no, let it go. When it comes to letting go of people and things, it doesn't require a big announcement. Simply make yourself less and less available.

Day 10

10 (ten)

Self-reliance, self-determination, rebirth, regeneration, wholeness, and infinite potential

Affirmation of the Day:

Things are getting better every day and I Am open to new possibilities.

Theme Song:

"Vibe For Me" by Aqyila

In order to show up fully in all aspects of your life, i.e., relationships, career, etc., you must embrace both sides of yourself. Remember the saying, there are two sides to a coin? Well there are two sides to you, also. Everything has a yin/yang flow. Without darkness, there is no light. To be whole is to accept and embody both your light and shadow-self.

The light-self is not necessarily always expressions of positivity. It represents your ego and how you present yourself to the outside world. It's the part of you that you spotlight for others to see and know you by.

There's another aspect to pay attention to here … the subconscious mind. The subconscious mind is not of focal awareness. It makes decisions on how you act or react without you actively thinking about it. It's able to do this by using stored memory of similar past events.

When the ego subdues the subconscious, the shadow is created. The shadow-self is the parts of you that are disowned and hidden from others. This can be a result of religious/spiritual beliefs, societal judgment, and/or your personal upbringing. This creates fear of judgment, fear of failure, gives you low self-esteem, and prevents you from living your authentic truth.

It's up to you to change the narrative and that's an inside job. Focus on raising your internal vibrations to match your external desires.

The human body has energy centers called chakras. Chakras are distributed throughout the body, with seven of the main chakras located along your spine. Your creative energy lies in your sacral chakra. This is the second energy center on the body, located about two inches below your belly button. It is the energetic home for your creative expressions, sensuality, and sexuality.

When you suppress your sensual side, you suppress your creativity. When you suppress your creativity, you lose your identity, forfeit your power, and follow the vision that other people have for your life.

Become aware of the part of you that you have disowned through moral judgment. Integrate your darkness into the light. Give credence to the most raw form of yourself and profess your true essence without guilt or shame. Be whole, in light and in darkness.

Activity:

It's shadow-work time! One of the most effective exercises is Ken Wilber's 3-2-1 Shadow Process. This practice is done by meditation.

The approach of this exercise is to first face it, then talk to it, and finally to be it. Conceptually, you will objectively reflect at a negative situation with another person in order to gain an alternative perspective in your thoughts and feelings. By doing so, you'll be able to readily recognize not only the difficulties you had with the person, but also gain clarity and insight on the mirrored disconnect that you have with yourself.

Here's the technique:

3. Face it.

Start by choosing a who. Then, close your eyes and visualize them. Once you can picture them entirely, use third person pronouns to describe the traits and qualities that are utterly bothersome to you. Say it out loud and don't hold back.

2. Talk to it.

Now it's time to communicate with them. All of the things you wish you would have said and all the questions you wanted to ask but didn't, do it now. Imagine their answers and say them out loud; respond accordingly. Keep the dialogue open until you feel a sense of contentment.

1. Be it.

Finally, become the other person that you've been in this dialogue with. Take on their traits and qualities you listed in step 3. Identify them as your own using I Am statements. (i.e. I Am envious, I Am jealous, I Am hurt).

Theoretically, if you find yourself in discomfort during this portion of the exercise, then you can assume these qualities belong to you and you've been suppressing them for one reason or another. Acknowledge them and actively begin to heal. Don't be too hard on yourself. Give yourself grace and compassion. Forgive yourself. Also, do the same for the other person you were focusing blame/shame on.

 *Journal Entry:*

Upon completion of the 3-2-1 Shadow Process, record your findings. Explain your experience in full detail. What was your biggest takeaway?

Day 11

11 (eleven)

Intuition, visualization, instinct, idealism, and empathy

Affirmation of the Day:

I Am connected to all around me through spiritual energy, love, and light.

Theme Song:

"Manifest" by Azaria

Do you remember that time you were hungry and craved a sandwich? You wanted it so bad that you could see it, smell it, and taste it even before having it. You then went to the kitchen, opened the refrigerator, and quickly snatched out all the ingredients you needed to prepare the best version of this sandwich you had yet to taste.

Finally, the ultimate sandwich creation is complete, and you take that first bite. You may have even done a little happy dance while your taste buds joined you in bliss. You transformed your situation from famine to fully satisfied … and your belly thanked you.

Believe it or not, you manifested your desired outcome through a process of visualization fueled by yearning. There's enormous power in visualization. The visual itself is just an image. The ization is the intention that fosters the bigger picture.

In order to see it, you first have to know it and believe it can happen. Just like you knew exactly what you wanted when you discovered you were hungry, define exactly what you want for your life. Get clear about it. Conceptualize it.

You have the ability to manifest all of your desires into your life. It's going to take some mental rehearsal, no doubt about that. The goal is to match your conscious mind with your subconscious. The conscious mind pretty much already knows what it wants. The subconscious, however, sometimes tries to trick the conscious mind through how it feels about your thoughts. Those feelings trump all. Emotion is energy-in-motion, it's what becomes your reality regardless of what you say or do. Pay attention to the energy where your vision is housed. Any negative emotions or thoughts that could block you from achieving your goals must be released.

Close your eyes and imagine yourself doing what you love for the rest of your life. What does it look like? What's the setting? Are you in your home, outside, or in a building? What do you smell? What sounds do you hear? What colors do you see? Are there other people around you? What are they doing? How are they benefiting from what you offer? Record your visualization experience.

Day 12

12 (twelve)

Creative exploration, creative self-expression, cooperation, inspired co-existence, and optimistic visualization

Affirmation of the Day:

All of my goals are crystal clear, and I maintain a detailed picture of what I desire.

Theme Song:

"I Am Woman" by Emmy Meli

Now that you've defined and refined your vision, let's unleash your creativity! One of the most effective ways to remain focused is to create something physical that reminds you of your goals and dreams. In your mind, it's merely a thought. Creating something physical to represent it, adding the sense of sight, makes it more tangible.

I created my latest vision board at the end of 2020. From a pile of old magazines gifted by my mother and grandmother, I cut out all the pictures and words that mirrored the goals and desires that I had for my life. Anything I didn't find in the magazines, I used Google and printed it out. I also found some pretty cool sparkly adhesive letters at Hobby Lobby.

Using a glue stick, I strategically placed each item on a thick white poster board until the board was completely full. It's one of my most prized art works. It's simply beautiful. Some of my favorite things on my board are; a woman clutching a microphone with her arm raised in the air, a woman meditating in nature next to the word Zen, and the phrase Lights, Camera, Impact. Oh yes, I cannot forget to mention that I outlined my board with money-print duct tape. Yes! Bring on the money vibes. I'm excited to share that most of what's on that board has already manifested. I think it's time for some new goals and I'm excited about that.

Oprah Winfrey, one of the world's wealthiest and prosperous African-American women, is a vision board enthusiast. She used the power of visualization to escape from the pits of poverty and is now globally recognized as the "Queen of All Media." She's also one of the greatest philanthropists in United States History. Oprah is a living legend.

Vision boards are one of the best visualization-manifestation tools. They help us create better objectives and stay focused on the prize. It's super important to have aspirations to achieve whatever you place on a vision board. Don't set yourself up for disappointment by over-reaching. That doesn't mean you can't dream big. But I am saying, don't forget the smaller steps you must first accomplish before reaching the grander outcome.

 Activity:

Create a vision board of your own. Grab some magazines, newspapers, and whatever else you can use to collect pictures and words. Let your creativity flow.

Journal Entry:

Pick one thing from your vision board to focus on. Commit to it and write about what you can do to accomplish it. Create a step-by-step-plan of action to execute it.

Day 13

13 (thirteen)

Sacred femininity, karmas, death of ego/old self, rebirth to spirit, production of tangible outcomes, and new firm foundations

Affirmation of the Day:

My higher-self guides me on the best path for growth each day.

Theme Song:

"Little Things" by India Arie

Thirteen is a very sacred number. Some would say that the number thirteen is bad luck. I would beg to differ. It's so misunderstood, something like the black sheep of the number family. It's a karmic number. Whatever you put out, the thirteen is going to send back around to you full circle. If there's a part of you that's not aligned with your true destiny, good ol' thirteen is definitely coming to teach you a hard lesson. This is the very reason why people give it such a bad rap. Who wants hard lessons, right? Yet, with great challenges come great rewards if you're willing to do the work.

Let's take a look at the moon. The moon is governed by sacred feminine energy. There are 13 moon cycles in a year that represent the 13 lunar menstruations of a woman's sacred womb. Menstruation is the process of the reproductive organs shedding what it no longer needs at the end of a cycle. You must do the very same with the things and people in your life that are no longer aligned with you.

A higher level of existence is what's calling your attention now. Let go of any uncertainty, hesitation, doubts, and fears. Surrender and allow nothing to hold you back. You can't build a new firm foundation by placing bricks on sticks. Dismantle your old self, bring death to the ego, and allow yourself to be reborn in spirit.

Allow yourself to fully feel today. When's the last time you had an ugly cry? I mean, that belting voice, scrunched up face, let it all out type of cry. Have that moment. Release any pent up tension you've been holding on to. Free yourself from the heavy load you've been carrying. You can go much further when you pack light.

 *Journal Entry:*

Create a two-column/thirteen row chart. In the left column identify and write 13 words that describe your ego. In the right column, replace those words with attributes of your higher self.

EGO	HIGHER SELF
BLAMING OTHERS	TAKING ACCOUNTABILITY
CONSTANT DRAMA	INNER PEACE

Day 14

14 (fourteen)

Personal freedom, consciousness, transformation, versatility, and worldly matters

Affirmation of the Day:

I Am free from any childhood conditions that once dimmed my light.

Theme Song:

"Don't Let It Go to Your Head" by Cleo Sol

The only thing that is constant in and of this world is change. Everything is constantly in motion even in stillness, including you. Your situations and circumstances are forever shifting. Nonetheless, sometimes you might feel stuck and unable to move in any direction.

The one thing that can keep you feeling stuck is an over-fixated mind. Focusing on the past or daydreaming way too much about the future robs you of the present moment. If this sounds like you, it's because of your preconceived expectations of what you think things should look like in your life rather than just being.

Cultivating the energy of mindfulness is the key to remaining aware of what's right in front of you. There are two parts to mindfulness, mind consciousness and stored consciousness. Mind consciousness is the state of being actively aware of the present moment. Stored consciousness is the base of thoughts and feelings, rooted in your past circumstances and experiences.

When your mind is operating in stored consciousness, emotions like fear, anger, and anxiety start to surface and can cause you to retreat. Carrying around unprocessed emotions can:

- Effect the way you think about yourself

- Effect how you react to stress

- Weigh heavily on your relationship with others

- Have some negative effect on your physical well-being.

All too often people are taught to bury the hurt and push past any pain. When the going gets really tough, some seek things to mask their reality like overindulging in harmful activities such as drinking and taking drugs. Over time, that does more damage than the initial strife. Break the cycle and let your feelings flow. Don't hold back, your feelings are valid.

Activity:

Think about the last time you were angry or anxious. Now close your eyes and put yourself back in the same situation and same setting. Visualize every detail as if it were happening all over again. Take note of where on your body you actually feel your emotions. Is your chest tight? Do you feel tension in your hips? What about heaviness in your feet?

Acknowledge your feelings. Connect with and understand your emotions. Then, recall and work through past traumas. You can use the 3-2-1 Shadow Process we did on Day 10 for this step. Lastly, release the emotions through intentional movement. Stretching, dancing, yoga, tai chi, or a simple walk in the park are all great options.

Journal Entry:

Repeat the above activity, changing the scenario a couple of times. Record what you found in your stored consciousness that you weren't aware of. Then list ways you can better manage your emotions and be more mindful.

Day 15

15 (fifteen)

Family ties, self-sacrifice, protection, acceptance, harmony, self-compassion, and healing

Affirmation of the Day:

I forgive others and myself for any past transgressions.

Theme Song:

"Keep The Faith" by Faith Evans

Give yourself a round of applause for making it halfway through your 30-day journey. You should already begin to feel a shift in your overall energy. Doesn't it feel amazing?

When you start becoming more aware of yourself, great life-altering things begin to emerge from the inside out. You'll get excited and immediately want to tell everyone especially those close to you like family and friends. You can't wait to share your awakening experience and newfound knowledge. Some may even plaster it all over social media, seeking instant gratification.

Whew! Let me first just say, been there done that. It almost never turns out the way you think. People get comfortable with the version of you they met 2, 3, and 10 years ago. They tend to want to keep you in that same energy and image, so you may not get the response you were looking for. This is why we must relinquish the need for outside validation.

Most of my childhood and young adult life, I idolized my father. He was my superman. I watched him overcome challenge after challenge, barely breaking a sweat. He worked hard, tirelessly, all the time. Come to think of it, I've never seen him cry. He had the same expectations for his children.

I aspired to be the perfect person that I viewed him to be. In school, I would play sports and join different organizations just to keep myself busy. I also thought this would make him proud. Every time I made the cut for a team I ran home just to tell him. To my surprise, he was never really excited about any of it. My dad showed up to two of my basketball games. When I didn't perform to his standards of a good player he stopped showing up. Apparently, he found it pointless if his daughter wasn't the star of the team. In response, I kept trying thing after thing in hopes he would finally celebrate me. That never happened.

As a result of all of this, as an adult, I became codependent in my intimate relationships. Through every partner, I was in search of love, admiration, and affirmation … the voids felt from within. You can imagine how those relationships ended. Yikes.

One day, sometime in my late 20's, I was having a phone conversation with my father. We were discussing relationship dynamics. I was interested in knowing his thoughts and feelings about a particular dynamic. I was always sort of anxious with him, especially when it came to his judgment of my character and life decisions. To my surprise, when I asked the question, his reply was, "La, why do you always ask me how I feel about your life? Your life is yours for a reason. Do what makes you happy and stop worrying about what other people think. If anybody has a problem with how you choose to live, then leave them where they are. You only get one life; live it how you want to."

At that moment, a huge weight was lifted from my shoulders. It was the most liberating thing he could have ever said to me. I felt free to be me.

Take away this: Your life is just that…yours. Your vision is yours alone, as well. It was given to you specifically because only you possess the unique gifts to make it happen. The clarity you have gained on your journey thus far is preparing you for something greater. Not everyone is going to see it, and that's okay.

Be careful and mindful not to project your truth, as if everyone should see it your way. Everyone has his or her own path. This isn't to say you're going to go it alone because you won't. Your help and support will come from people who resonate with your story and your ultimate goal, in due time. Find peace in losing people in your path. Everyone can't go where you're going. And respectfully, everyone doesn't deserve to ride along.

Expressing your authentic self is still important and shouldn't be repressed. Moreover, the greater message to convey is motivating others to find and live their truth. Release the idea that we are all supposed to think, act, and be the same. Focus your energy on accepting yourself, accepting others where they are, and exploring ways to be collaborative with all the beautiful gifts around you.

In order to invite newness into your life, you first must let the things and people that are no longer serving you die. Start your first journal entry with "I commit to 30 Days of Me. During this 30-day devotion to myself, I release…" Then, make a list of all the things and energies that have been weighing heavily on you. (i.e. fear of judgment, procrastination, need for validation).

Once your release list is complete, make another list to fill the void of what you just emptied. Begin with, "I reclaim my power. I invite back into my space…" (i.e., self-acceptance, progression, or self-confidence).

Journal Entry:

Write about a time you shared some amazing news with a friend or family member and didn't get the response you expected. How did it make you feel?

Then write about how you can show up and celebrate other people when they share good news with you.

Day 16

16 (sixteen)

Introspection, perfectionism, analytical wisdom, spiritual wisdom, philosophy, and karmic entanglements

Affirmation of the Day:

I Am allowing myself to surrender and open my heart to new possibilities.

Theme Song:

"Self Care" (extended version) by Savannah Christina

Pay attention to your intuition today. Those gut feelings you get that something isn't quite right show up for a reason, so don't ignore them. These inklings come to warn you of danger and destruction.

The word of the day is elevation. In order to move to higher grounds, you'll need to summon your courage and willpower. Deal with any present obstacles you may be facing in your life right now. If you are struggling with a karmic love affair or financial struggles, get a handle on them now. Trust your instincts in the process.

We've all been hurt by a lover in the past. Some of us may even be going through heartbreak in real time. Let's take a deep reflective dive into these relationships. Has this past pain closed you off to the idea that unconditional love is available to you? Is it hard for you to open your heart and trust others now?

Perceiving and digesting our past experiences through a lens of negativity can stop us from experiencing the life our hearts truly desire. What if we replaced the nouns in our wound stories with a character trait? What would that look like? Because truth be told, the lessons you learned in life so far were all in accordance with your life plan/purpose. Nothing is personal; everything is energetic. Forgive yourself and others that may have hurt you.

Now, take a reflective look at the relationship you have with money. Do this by asking yourself similar questions from the people-connection shadow work. How do you feel about money? What emotions arise when you talk about money? What recurring thoughts and patterns do you deal with when it comes to matters of finance? Answering these questions will better inform you of your relationship with money.

People aren't bad with money. Some simply have unhealthy relationships with money. Instead of governing their money, they allow their money to control them. This can manifest as feeling like a slave to money, financial shame, money anxiety, or avoiding financial responsibilities altogether.

Factors like cultural conditioning, religion, and childhood upbringing are some of the many things that can have an impact on your relationship with money. Did you grow up hearing, "Money doesn't grow on trees" or "Money is the root of all evil?" These statements play in your subconscious mind. Then, habits are built around those feelings to protect yourself as if you have to fight to get money and fight to not let it overpower you.

Now that the elements that impact our relationship with money have been identified, let's cultivate a good one. Start by identifying your current status with money and how it makes you feel. Next, identify what a healthy money relationship looks like to you. Then, adopt those thoughts and implement practices to keep you in that same mindset.

Activity:

Create a financial staircase. On a blank sheet of paper, draw a 7-step staircase. Label each step with a manageable financial milestone. Note each milestone with one month following the next, giving you a 7-month timespan.

Then, write yourself a check. How much money do you want to see in your bank account in 7 months? If you don't have a checkbook, print a dummy-check from Google images or draw one of your own. Place both items on your vision board.

Journal Entry:

We've all had our fair share of toxic relationships. Whether we were the contributing party, or we allowed our partner to spew negativity all over our life, we must have some sense of accountability in the role we played.

Write about a time you ignored all the red flags. Then write about ways you can commit to being more aware of your intuition.

Day 17

17 (seventeen)

Business management, problem solving, strategy, thought-manifestation, and material acquisition

Affirmation of the Day:

All my thoughts and efforts lead me to the success I desire.

Theme Song:

"In my bag" by Thuy

We've done enough destruction to the old self for now. Anytime you empty/release portions of your life, you must then replenish those spaces with all the positive things you intend.

It's time to get your business affairs in order. The number 17 contains all attributes of the 1,7, and 8. The essence of their sum simplified (8), represents effective and efficient strategies to problem solving.

Now that you've identified your innate gifts and skills you bring to the world, apply them in a manner that supports your highest good and the good of others. Be intentional when it comes to material acquisitions. You want to ensure you're building things of lasting value that benefit everyone for years to come. The value of all you do is measured by the impact you make.

Gear your thoughts into an abundance mindset. This calls for a well thought out master plan to achieve your highest goals. Once you define the vision, you can then center your attention on what tools you're going to need to begin the construction process.

Every day is an opportunity to reestablish where to invest your energy, time, and resources. There is no final destination. Success doesn't have an arrival; there's always room for improvement. Ask yourself, "How can what I am building or desire to build be better?"

Journal Entry:

Most people define and acknowledge someone's legacy at the point of death. Your legacy is not death … it's life. It's not 5 or 10 years ago … it's now. The footprints of your path now and what you construct in your life today are what your legacy will be tomorrow.

What's your legacy? Envision it. In detail, write about what it looks like as if it has already come to fruition. What did you build? What impact did you make?

Then write about ways you can start showing up in your day-to-day, laying brick by brick, to work towards building it as you see it.

Day 18

18 (eighteen)

Inner-strength, assertiveness, empathy, tolerance, refinement, philanthropy, and humanitarianism

Affirmation of the Day:

My heart is constantly growing bigger with compassion for others.

Theme Song:

"Positive" by Erica Campbell

    Knowing your energy is half the equation. The other half is owning your energy and giving what you have to offer to this world. The outcome should lead you to do something bigger than your-self. Now that you know your what, let's determine your why.

    Your why is what solves a problem. It brings about peace and harmony to a specific subject matter. On day 17, we began visualizing what our legacy looks like. Now let's explore and create some tangible fillers to start making the mark. Ask yourself, "Who am I helping? What cause am I sup-porting? What's one problem I want to solve? How do I use my unique gifts in this case? What changes and impact can I make?"

    Take a look back at the attributes of the numbers 1 and 8. The 1 is a representation of the self-sufficient leader within you. The 8 summons you to be an action-prone doer. Collectively, the 9 (1+8) commands you to do it for the people. The beautiful thing is, when and what you manifest for the greater good of others, you are rewarded with the same type of energy through blessings ten times over.

When considering my career path as a young adult, being a Master Numerologist was never a part of the plan. And if I'm being completely transparent, I didn't have a plan. I was good at just about anything that I put my mind to. It also helped that I am a very fast learner.

My resume is quite long. I bounced from one job to the next. Sadly, I eventually despised all of them because they just didn't feel right. It was something about waking up at the same time every day, clocking in at the same time, clocking out at the same time, going home to tend to my family duties, and then going to bed just to wake up and do it all over again that didn't sit right with me. I felt like a robot.

Then, in 2014, I had a major epiphany and awakening through the reflection of my children. My oldest son, Cameron, has autism. He was labeled non-verbal until age seven. Cameron is a number enthusiast. Before he was able to utter his first words, he manipulated toys and objects to create a number or number sequence. When he began speaking, his words were most times associated with a number. Even things he would build with Legos or other toys had something to do with num-bers.

It finally hit me. I began doing research on numbers and stumbled across numerology. I discovered that numbers have a deeper meaning and there are divine messages attached to them. I became just as fascinated with them as he was.

Through the study of numerology techniques, I was awakened to my life's purpose. My devotion is to awaken others to their purpose using the same techniques in which I discovered my own.

I'm on Life Path 7. Life Path 7 represents The Truth Seeker and The Teacher. The 7's aim is to explore and connect the dots between the physical realm and spiritual realm. Those on this path are given the task to spread its wisdom to whoever crosses their path. I accept my truth. I honor my truth. Because I live my truth, it has afforded me wealth and abundance beyond physical measure.

Activity:

Find your life path number. Google Life Path Calculator, then enter your date of birth.

LP 1 - The Independent/Leader	LP 7 - The Truth Seeker/Intellectual
LP 2 - The Peacemaker	LP 8 - The Executive
LP 3 - The Creative	LP 9 - The Humanitarian
LP 4 - The Worker Bee/Builder	LP 11 - The Spiritual Messenger/Intuitive
LP 5 - The Adventurer	LP 22 - The Master Builder/Architect
LP 6 - The Lover	LP 33 - The Master Teacher

Journal Entry:

What's the recurring theme in your past connections and circumstances? How have they affected how you see yourself and the ability to achieve goals? Write two other positive perspectives or outcomes to take the place of your negative outlook.

Day 19

19 (nineteen)

Self-determination, drive, enthusiasm, motivation, opportunities, power, and influence

Affirmation of the Day:

I approach each day embracing new opportunities to grow and learn.

Theme Song:

"Beautiful" by Kierra Sheard

Being independent, self-determined, feeling indestructible, and powerful gives you a sense of meaning and worth. This is actually where being the most cautious, mindful, and aware of the energy we exude comes into play.

Don't let it go to your head. This new surge of authority can cause you to abuse your power, especially in leadership roles. Be careful not to be too pushy. Be in control of you and your own life. You're only the boss of yourself. Attempting to dictate the thoughts, ideas, and actions of others is a violation of their free will and detours them from their true passions and purpose.

If your vision includes leading other people, focus on how you can do so in a fair and collaborative way that results in a win-win for all. Be open-minded about exploring others' perspectives and open your eyes to see the new opportunities that can be birthed from them. Not all opportunities presented to you are going to look exactly like what you are looking for. Nonetheless, if you can envision the potential for evolution, then take it and run with it. Mold it and grow with it until it becomes exactly what you need.

Everyone has gifts, talents, skills, passions, and purpose. Allow space for the people in your life to express and give all of what they have to offer without limitation and judgment. Each piece to the puzzle is uniquely crafted, but together, they all fit for a much larger, beautiful picture.

Journal Entry:

Write about a leader you worked with that had a negative impact on you. What were their motives? How did it affect you?

Then, write about a leader that impacted you in a positive way. What inspirations did they spark in you? How can you apply what they taught you about effective leadership?

Day 20

20 (twenty)

Comprehension, receptivity, coexistence, teamwork, companionship, and negotiations

Affirmation of the Day:

I Am compassionate, understanding, and accepting towards all life forms.

Theme Song:

"It's My Time" by Kelly Price

The number 2 represents your soul mission in life. It's about maintaining your partnership with the Universe and managing your relationships with others while walking in your purpose. The 0 symbolizes the Universe itself. Together, the 20's expression mirrors the development and enhancement of your spirituality and the application of your life purpose to do great work.

The number 20 also radiates an abundance of divine feminine energy. At this time, your intuition and inner wisdom should be unlocked and at its zenith. If there was ever a time to trust yourself, it's now. Take another self-inventory of yourself and your surroundings. Heightened vibrations and bright lights attract bugs. Be aware of the things and people trying to attach themselves to you.

By this time, you should be able to recognize who is in your corner and who is not. You've been in isolation for 20 days now. Pay attention to the people who feel slighted or who shame you for not being as easily accessible. Take note of those who don't understand and respect your time away for self-care and adjust accordingly. Stand in your divine feminine power and receive only what and who replenishes you.

If you are finding yourself in an overly sensitive, emotional state of being or easily influenced by other people's feelings and circumstances, don't be afraid to wave that red flag. Take a step back and determine what energies actually belong to you and what doesn't. Shed the weight of all that is draining your energy and dimming your light.

Let's indulge in some art therapy. Meditate for 20 minutes without focusing on anything in particular. Pay attention to and listen to what presents itself to you. Then draw or paint how you feel. It doesn't have to make sense. Just let your art utensil flow.

Journal Entry:

Self-care isn't selfish. Yet, it's neglected far too often. Some people are more concerned with contributing to everyone else's happiness, even at the expense of neglecting their own needs.

People-pleasing gives a false sense of feeling needed and plays on your ego. Initially, the reaction you get from putting others first can give you a false sense of value. A lot of times you don't realize your cup is empty until you're drained.

Write about your personal experiences (past or present) with people-pleasing. Then, come up with some healthy boundaries to put in place to honor yourself.

Day 21

21 (twenty-one)
Inspiration, creative expression, progress, success, achievements, and optimism

Affirmation of the Day:
I deserve the space and freedom to do all the things I love.

Theme Song:
"Healing Is Not My Purpose" by Toni Jones

Your life is heading in a groundbreaking direction. Let's just take a moment to stop, breathe, and rejoice for a moment. Newness is all around you. Don't question whether you're ready or not, just be open. Let go of your need to hold on to past attempts or try to control the future. Simply "just be" right now in this moment … and smile while you're present.

We've done a lot of unpacking and even began the process of rebuilding. The work you've put in thus far has given you a clearer perspective, some amazingly fresh ideas, and may even have presented some potential opportunities for you. You've discovered your creativity to be limitless and boundless, and you're creating with more intention than ever. Your thoughts are filled with love, joy, peace, and gratitude. You've vowed to express your authentic truth and hold space for others to do the same. It's just beautiful. You're just beautiful.

Make sure you keep that same energy. Like energy attracts like energy. The law of attraction isn't simply speaking things into existence. Instead, what you are is what you become a magnet to. Therefore, your thoughts and actions must be a vibrational match to the things you call. That's what determines the outcome. Continue to be optimistic about your future, allowing it to unfold one cycle at time. A "glass half full" attitude and mindset are what's going to help you achieve all of your goals.

I joined Clubhouse in January 2021. After about three strong weeks on the app, I collaborated with a group of like-minded individuals with the common goal to help other people push their personal and business brand.

Collectively, we had a desire to do something bigger than and outside of ourselves. That paid off! We came to run one of the largest networking and engagement rooms on the platform, drawing the attention of entertainers, entrepreneurs, small and corporate businesses.

Once official clubs started formulating on the app, I joined the I Am Creator club, where I stood in as the team's Master Numerologist. Daily topics ranged from law of attraction, manifestation, to mindset — and other related topics. Our mission and purpose was to help guide people to the highest and best version of themselves.

Clubhouse helped me get out of my own way and help others. I had already mastered the art of my independence. My next level up was finding the balance between keeping my own cup full and having the energy to pour into others.

I used my voice to push other people and their brand. I showered them with encouraging words and genuine support. In return, I reaped great rewards.

As a result of Clubhouse I have:

- Been published in a Saudi magazine
- Been a guest on many podcasts
- Been a guest speaker at a church
- Been keynote speaker for a couple of international summits

I am also now a #1 Bestselling Author. Blessings are still pouring down on me. I'm excited to experience all of what's yet to come.

Take some time today to commemorate your wins, big and small. Celebrate how far you've come. By doing so, you'll cultivate the vibe needed to create and attract more of that same energy.

Practicing gratitude and celebrating your wins is a game changer! Think of each small win as a brick to the building you are constructing. What are you grateful for? Where are you winning in life? Write a letter of gratitude. Then go out and have some fun today. You deserve it.

Day 22

22 (twenty-two)

Foundations, security, discipline, focus, future, material plane, idealism, ambition, and cooperation

Affirmation of the Day:

I Am capable of overcoming any challenges the future has for me.

Theme Song:

"The King's Affirmation" by Iniko

Yesterday's play day should have been just what you needed to refresh. Hopefully, you feel rejuvenated and ready to dive back in. Now, let's get back to building. Master Number 22 brings just that type of energy. It represents the Master Builder/Architect. The 22 is one of the most powerful of all numbers. So, buckle up … here we grow!

With clearly defined goals, coupled with unwavering ambition, you can achieve all you set out to accomplish. When idealizing your goals, always check in with yourself. Ask yourself, "What do I desire to achieve? Why is this important to me?" Call your personal power into action. Awaken your confidence and willpower. Always follow your heart and intuition in all scenarios.

Know that in this process of rebuilding, there is no such thing as perfection. So, release any ideas of perfectionism. Sometimes things will not pan out in the exact manner you envisioned. Your only job is to stay in flow and trust the process. As long as you continue on your life path to fulfill your life purpose, then nothing has gone wrong and nothing will go wrong. In your plan to be all that you can be, there's always a solution to every challenging equation.

Speaking of plans, have you ever heard of S.M.A.R.T. Goals? S.M.A.R.T. Goals is an effective goal-setting technique to help you map out a plan to reach a desired destination. The acronym stands for Specific, Measurable, Attainable, Relevant, and Timely. This technique guides you in taking small steps towards the bigger picture. Here's an example of how it works:

SPECIFIC:

Goal: I want to lose weight

How: I will replace soda with water and workout three times per week. You can also set specific days and times.

We all have dreams and goals but most are generalized and vague. Your goal must be clear and well defined. You can only get to where you want by defining precisely how you will get there.

MEASURABLE:

Goal: I want to lose 10 pounds

Scale your progress along the way! Set three small goals within the bigger goal. First, shoot for losing the first 3 pounds. Then, shoot for 3 more. Now, you're ready to close it out with the final 4!

Tracking the progress of your goal is part of what's going to keep you motivated to see it all the way through. You can set milestones to celebrate when you achieve them and re-evaluate when you don't. Break it down into manageable pieces. If you don't have a way to measure it, you're likely to lose your ambition and quit.

ATTAINABLE:

Unrealistic Goal: I want to lose 10 pounds in 2 days

Attainable Goal: I want to lose 3 pounds per week

Make sure the goals you set for yourself are possible for where you are right now. Your goals should not be impossible; they should be challenging and achievable. Setting yourself up for failure by going beyond your bounds of possibilities will only make you miserable and feel like a failure.

RELEVANT:

Idea: I think that I want to learn software engineering.

Why: The pay is good.

Unless your field of study is engineering and/or the likes of, this would be time consuming and quite frankly a waste of time. Ask yourself, "Does this even make sense?" I know for me, it wouldn't. When money is the motive, oftentimes there's a neglect of passion.

Your goals should be relevant to the direction you want your life and career to take. A common issue many people have is pursuing the wrong goals. Achieving the wrong goals will have you feeling like you haven't accomplished anything.

TIMELY:

Recall a time your boss gave you a task and needed it completed ASAP! It was a Wednesday afternoon when he/she assigned it to you and then gave you a deadline of Friday by 2:00 pm.

Your plans must have a deadline too, otherwise you'll have unlimited time to achieve them and are more likely to procrastinate. If you're working on a deadline, your sense of urgency increases.

Activity:

On a piece of paper or poster board, draw a 5 column chart and label the top S.M.A.R.T. Using the S.M.A.R.T. goals technique, outline something major you want to achieve.

Activity:

Take out a piece of paper. At the bottom of the page, draw a figure to represent you and where you are right now. At the top of the page, draw or use words to represent where you desire to be. The distance between the two represents space and time. Fold the paper in half to allow the top and bottom to merge as one. Now, you and your desires occupy the same space. Set this paper aside in a safe place to use later for a vision board activity.

GOAL:				
S	**M**	**A**	**R**	**T**

Journal Entry:

Our beliefs and how we manage them determine our actions. Our actions, in turn, determine our results. What are your personal beliefs? How well do you manage your personal beliefs? How are they relevant to your goals?

Day 23

23 (twenty-three)

Whimsical freedom, companionship, development (personal and spiritual), eloquence, and fulfillment

Affirmation of the Day:

I Am strengthening my relationships with others while also maintaining my personal freedom.

Theme Song:

"Golden" by Jill Scott

Interdependence should be a familiar term by now, although the majority of our efforts have been to first learn independence. Now, let's talk about what that actually looks like. There are two keys to the door of building interdependent relationships. The first key is to be aware and mindful of who you are, even before entering one. The second key is to allow room and opportunity for the other person to do the same thing. When you start any relationship this way, it allows for the development of a safe space for both parties to learn and grow together without the fear of losing their identity or feeling controlled.

Interdependency requires acceptance of self and others. Be adaptable. You might actually learn something new by opening up to different perspectives aside from your own. We know the number 2 to represent partnerships. The number 3 hones in on our creative expressions. If the two numbers were to compose a duet, it would be titled, Free In Love. This frequency has a companionable essence that expresses its sense of personal freedom while being beautifully intertwined.

All is well in fair exchanges of energy. Use your talents and creativity to bring joy and peace to yourself and others. When considering what you desire your relationship with others to look and feel like, get real with yourself. Be transparent. Set yourself free to express and impress your authentic truth. You're at your best when you are

Journal Entry:

Healthy interdependent relationships involve a balance of both parties honoring themselves first while being present in the relationship and meeting each other's emotional and physical needs in a meaningful and purposeful way.

Write about what your relationship looks like now. What are some ways you can elevate them to higher levels? If you're not currently involved, using the ideas of interdependency, write about the perfect relationship for you. Go into detail of what it looks like, what it feels like, and how you and your partner support one another.

24 (twenty-four)

The body, health, beauty, overall well-being, passion, integrity, security, goals, and desires

Affirmation of the Day:

I Am grateful for excellent strength, great health, and a sound mind.

Theme Song:

"I Am" by Iamjustjoy Anderson

As humans, we were given choice and free will. Sometimes it's a blessing, other times it feels like a curse. Why is it so much easier to not do the right thing? This is where willpower and integrity need to kick into gear. Living a healthy lifestyle involves choice and action. Similar to the principles of the law of attraction, you first have to believe it, choose to be it, and then do it.

We live in a world satisfied by the quick and easy — instant gratification. We value material goods and fast/convenient foods, welcoming illnesses, and diseases into our bodies. Then, we look for quick fixes through some company's magic pill or drink in hopes that it'll reverse the damage we've done. We want everything fast, always searching for the quick fix. That doesn't always work.

Near the end of February 2019, I had the biggest health scare of my life. There were several contributing factors to this scare, including being a heavy smoker and having an unhealthy diet. The emotional and mental strain from grieving my father's death put the icing on the cake. His transition hit me so hard, I went through a period of depression.

One afternoon I drove my children to their favorite restaurant to get the usual. That is our weekly routine depending on whether or not they have a week of good behavior at home and school. We order the same thing every single time. But something quite eerie happened this time. The order total was different. Without giving it a second thought, I drove to the checkout window, paid what was due, and tossed the receipt in the center console. Cameron yelled out, "Mommy, 13! 13!" It sparked my curiosity, so I grabbed the receipt and O-M-G. In big bold numbers at the top it read 1313. As my eyes scrolled down the receipt I notice our order was placed on register #13, at time-stamp 13:13, four (4) items, totaling $13.13. My jaw dropped, and I instantly felt ill. I thought the feeling would eventually go away, but it didn't. My chest was tight, my stomach was in knots, and I had a tingling sensation in my thighs. I didn't wait around much longer; I called a doctor the very next morning.

Upon the doctors' diagnosis, I was obese, pre-diabetic, my blood pressure was through the roof, and I had some abnormal growths in my lady parts. After getting an ultrasound at my OB/GYN it was confirmed I had a pretty bad case of fibroid tumors. The medical professionals suggested pharmaceutical medication and putting me under the knife. Yes, surgery. I wasn't having it.

My spirit told me to take a holistic healing approach. At the time, I had no clue what that would entail but I trusted my spirit. I made the decision that I was going to completely stop everything.

On March 1st, I stopped consuming all solid foods and stopped smoking cold turkey. The game plan was to water-fast for three days to detox my body and then slowly reintroduce raw fruits and veggies. The Universe had other plans.

On day three of my fast, a friend of mine randomly sent me a YouTube video. I clicked on it, and a woman wearing the most beautiful African garment and headdress said, "Ladies, we are under spiritual warfare. I need all of my Goddesses to fast with me beginning March 1st through the Spring Equinox on March 21st." Again, another jaw-dropping moment.

No one knew about my medical conditions or the fact that I was fasting. I took that as a message from the Universe telling me that I can cancel my thoughts of fasting for only three days. It summoned my discipline for a 21-day fast. I was obedient despite feeling like I was dying. It was hard to fathom going that long without food.

On day two, my body started experiencing shock, and I was having dizzy spells and double vision. It got so bad that I sat my children down and asked them who they would want to live with if something happened to me. After they gave me their answer, I made peace with it and made the conscious decision to move forward and trust that the Universe was going to provide all that was needed regardless of the outcome.

For 21 days and 21 nights, I consumed only spring water and herbal tea. I shopped at local apothecaries to purchase all the raw herbs I needed. I was definitely no herbalist guru, but my spirit led me to everything I needed. I also had the help of the storeowners to educate me on the proper mixing of herbs specific to my needs.

Along with an herbal regimen, I did yoga daily, breathwork, sunbathing, sun-gazing, mediation, stretching, and Tai chi. I even put filters on all the faucets in my home and changed the filter in the furnace. I wouldn't brush my teeth with tap water. I used spring water as much as I could for anything that required water. While taking a shower, I visualized the water soaking up all the ailments of my body and then releasing them down the drain.

By day six, I started to glow and others noticed it as well. The owner of one of the apothecaries I frequented started randomly gifting me and supporting my healing journey. Each time I walked through the door she had something for me. Whether it was a custom-crafted body butter, a gallon of alkaline water, or a bundle of rolled herbs to smoke, I was always in awe and grateful.

I completed the entire 21 days. I felt the best that I had ever felt my entire life. My skin was flawless; I lost thirty-something pounds and had an abundance of energy.

On day 26, I returned back to the doctor for a follow-up exam. When the doctor laid eyes on me, she could barely recognize who I was. A week later, my results were in. The doctor called and said, "La, what did you do?"

I replied, "What do you mean?"

"We couldn't find anything. Everything we discussed before is just gone," she said.

In the most peaceful voice I declared, "I followed my spirit."

Please note that I am sharing this, not for the purpose of stating that you should do a 21-day fast or any type of fast for that matter. I encourage you to follow your spirit and also consult with your health care provider, whether that be a physician or holistic practitioner. Every path is different.I put my path on my website for you to take a look.

It's important that we take care of our physical body. It is the temple in which the soul resides. You only get one. The better you care for it, the more potential for longevity you afford it to operate at optimal levels in order to carry out your life assignment and live a full, happy, and enjoyable life.

Activity:

Do 30 minutes of movement today.

- Take a walk

- Yoga

- Hiking

- Swimming

- Dance aerobic

- Running

Journal Entry:

When was the last time you had a routine checkup and what were the results? What lifestyle changes can you implement today to begin the journey of a healthier and happier you?

Day 25

25 (twenty-five)

Curiosity, discovery, ancient wisdom, shifts to new levels, grace, mindfulness, and thoughtfulness

Affirmation of the Day:

My spiritual self is always evolving and shifts with grace towards my highest good.

Theme Song:

"Extraordinary Being" by Emeli Sande

As a co-creator of your life, you have a deciding hand in how you experience your reality, who you allow in it, what you allow in it, what you follow, and how you lead.

The wisdom gained through your past experiences and connections with other people has granted knowledge of self. Yet, the work is never completely done. There is no end-all, be-all in healing and learning. We must always remain reflective students of life. Connect with your ancient wisdom and innate deeper knowledge. Explore what new ideas and possibilities are awaiting your discovery.

On day 13, we began working through building solid foundations. You may notice that, between then and now, your perspective and goals have shifted slightly, or maybe even drastically. That's a testament that you are evolving in real time. As you migrate to higher levels, the energy around you has no other choice but to transform with you. Allow it. Stay in flow.

As you continue to recast your life, remain open to new mindset developments and an updated heart's desire. The Universe is always shaking things up. Have you been considering a new career? Has your outlook on relationships changed any? Or maybe you've unveiled a higher soul mission. Whatever evolution you're going through, I bid you well, butterfly. Set yourself free from that cocoon.

Journal Entry:

   In all that you consider, seek your answers from within. Indulge in a 25-minute meditation, visualizing yourself in your highest physical form. What do you look like? What are
you wearing? What are you doing? How do you feel? Record your vision.

Day 26

26 (twenty-six)

Material accumulation, wealth, financial abundance, business-oriented matters relating to society, and encouragement

Affirmation of the Day:

Money comes to me in expected and unexpected ways.

Theme Song:

"Everywhere" by Chloe x Halle

Your mindset is your mental bank account. When you change your perception of money and how you feel about money, you tend to overcome financial challenges with more ease and make better financial choices. The power of positive thinking when it comes to money makes all the difference.

Keep your faith rooted in knowing you will always be provided for. View the outcome of your intended money goals through an optimistic lens. As a matter of course, things will turn out in your favor.

The number 26 presents opportunities for financial abundance and financial freedom. Law of attraction requires action, so the abundance mindset is only a portion of the work to be done. You must remain collaborative with the vision of your desires.

Whether you have $8,000 in debt or $80,000, it can be atoned for. Even if you have a 400 credit score now, there's always an opportunity to raise it through the roof. You first have to acknowledge and recognize all financial mishaps are fixable. Look for opportunities to leverage financial gain instead of only seeing roadblocks.

Start shaping your financial goals. To set any goal, you must first know your current status. What's your annual income? What are you monthly expenses? Do you know your FICO score? Debts?

Now determine some financial goals that are tangible for you to reach in the near future. How much would you like to make annually? How can you increase your income? Have you considered asking your boss for a raise? Have you been thinking about starting a business or side hustle?

While focusing on getting your financial matters in order, don't overwhelm yourself with debt elimination. Find a financial balance. Balance fosters stability. Make sure you include saving and gifting into your plan.

Activity:

Everyone is entitled to a free credit report every 12 months from all three major consumer-reporting agencies (Equifax, Experian, and Transunion). Pull and print your free report and FICO score from annualcreditreport.com.

Then, create a budget and S.M.A.R.T. Goal plan of action to reach your financial goals.

GOAL:				
S	M	A	R	T

Journal Entry:

We all have a kryptonite when it comes to spending money. What's yours? How can you use your personal power and resiliency to prevail over your arch nemesis and gain control over your money?

Day 27

27 (twenty-seven)

Spiritual awareness, ego death, empathic healing, compassion, and tolerance

Affirmation of the Day:

I Am an eternal and infinite being with the ability to tap into source energy at any time.

Theme Song:

"Good Morning Gorgeous" by Mary J. Blige

Everything is finally coming together, right? Or it's at least starting to make sense. On this 27th day, take another moment to reflect on where this 30-day process has taken you up to this point. You're nearing the end of this me journey. Now let's prepare for the we movement. Shift your energy and focus on bridging the gap between self and all of humanity.

On today, the number 2 calls for cooperation. The number 7 warrants you to tap into your spiritual essence. Altogether, the number 9 (2+7) says it's time to tie up any loose ends and cut any dangling cords.

You've learned and discovered so much about yourself. Most of your talents and gifts have come to the forefront with great clarity.

These are the very words I wished someone said to me as a teen and young adult. I lived a life of conformity and control for so long that I didn't know who I was. At every turn in my life there were all these expectations of me.

In 2014, I hit the pause button on everything and everybody. I'd had enough. At this point, I felt like I hit rock bottom. I was tired of having one failed relationship after another. I was exhausted from bouncing from job to job, trying to stay afloat in life. In my Beyonce voice, I said, "World, stop!" And it did. I quit my job via voicemail and never looked back. I'd recently had a bad breakup, so that was already out of the way.

I sat in meditation for hours. On one hand, I regretted what I did, but only because I was worried about how I was going to pay my bills and care for my children. On the other hand, I was relieved and felt a sense of liberty. Before long, my spirit began to speak to me. I felt a sudden urge to paint.

If you've learned anything about me in this book, you know I don't disobey my spirit. I went to the nearest arts and crafts store and purchased a cart full of art supplies like I was a master painter or something. You'd think I'd be a little frugal with my money considering I just quit my job, right? Nope.

When I returned home with all my new art supplies, I got busy. To my surprise, my masterpiece didn't come out half bad. Moreover, the best part was how good it felt to paint. It was so spiritually therapeutic. By my third painting, I was selling them.

In another meditation I recalled my childhood love for jewelry making. As a child, I used to enjoy making necklaces and bracelets with colorful acrylic beads. Some beads had letters engraved on them, which were used to make words or names.

I made another trip to the craft store. However, this time I wanted to create jewelry with more meaning and purpose. Instead of acrylic beads, I chose healing stones, also known as gemstones. Yes, you guessed it. When I made it back home, I got busy.

Just as I envisioned, I unlocked another outlet. The jewelry making process was mentally therapeutic to me. Something about it slows down my thoughts, enabling me to digest them in real time. This discovery was almost surreal. My mind naturally runs a million miles per minute. I kept at it, and now I'm a gemstone jewelry designer with my own jewelry line.

The third time I took a deep meditative dive, I recalled my love for poetry. My initial connection with rhythmical composition was discovered somewhere around the 8th grade. This was when school started to become challenging. Not the work itself, but the peer pressure from other students took a toll on me. Often times I wrote poems to express my emotions.

Back then, I never made anything of my poems. When I finished writing one, it became wadded-up paper in the trash bin.

However, this meditation reignited my passion for the pen and led me on a trip to the dollar store to buy a fresh notepad. When I returned home, once again I put my emotions on the paper.

My first love was spoken word poetry. I loved watching artist perform their pieces live. It was such an eclectic vibe. Prior to my reconnection with the pen, it was uncharted territory for me. So when I finished writing my poem, I dared to recite it out loud. I pulled out my phone and recorded myself. After about fifty takes, I finally had a decent recording that I was satisfied with.

Spontaneously, I reach out to a local artist who also happens to be an international spoken word artist, musician, and rapper. I sent him my recording and asked him for some constructive criticism. He said, "I viewed it. But I won't tell you what I think until you come perform it for me live at my next show on Tuesday."

It was Thursday y'all! I had only four days to memorize the entire poem and gain enough courage to get on stage and perform it. I've never been one to turn down any challenge, so I stepped up to the plate. For the first time ever, I was going to be on stage reciting a poem … my poem, "Parentless Child."

I rehearsed day and night, literally down to the second that it was time for me to perform. I was as nervous as ever. It wasn't stage fright, however. I was more concerned about the crowd's receptivity and reaction to the emotional damage that I was about to wail into the microphone.

I was the second to the last act that night. Watching the other artists express themselves freely and confidently helped calm my nerves. Everyone was phenomenal. I could see myself through every word that was spoken and every note that was played.

Then, the time finally came for me to spill my guts and speak my truth. I clenched the mic as tight as I could and went for it. I gave it all I had, allowing the vibrations of my words to echo all the bottled-up emotions I had been carrying since childhood.

Two minutes later, I received a standing ovation. The next week I was on the road to perform out of state. I shocked myself yet again.

Moral of the story: move forward with confidence in yourself and your abilities. Trust your inner wisdom and exercise faith in your convictions. The next level of your journey is learning to be selfless with the gifts you were given. It's time to present them to the world. Owning your talents and mastering your crafts are the only way to achieve your soul's higher purpose. We need you.

 *Journal Entry:*

Your ego springs into action when it feels like it has to protect you from something. It's the very thing that can keep you from presenting your gifts to the world. It doesn't want to fail, be judged, or be limited. In response, it sometimes holds you back from showing up at all.

What's your ego's sore spot? What are some ways you can start letting your guard down?

Day 28

28 (twenty-eight)

Conviction, adaptability, diplomacy, luck, universal law of karma, and gratitude

Affirmation of the Day:

I Am grateful for the blessings in my life, both big and small.

Theme Song:

"Closer" by Goapele

Today is all about focusing on what you have, rather than what you don't have. Give attention and praise for what's actually working the way you want. Also, know that all things are in place — including you — for you to succeed in life. You're exactly where you need to be.

Aside from the affirmation of the day, practice other positive affirmations today. Regular use of them reprograms your mind into believing all these statements you recite repeatedly. They motivate you to concentrate on you, act on your goals, change your negative thought patterns, and help boost your confidence. Call to all the greatness that has yet to enter your reality. Speak it as if it has already come to pass.

The energy of the number 28 implores you to be generous with all the wealth you've obtained, including your wealth of knowledge. The more you give, the more you receive. Consider possible collaborations today. Remember, you are responsible for the power you bring to any dynamic. Focus on the strengths you bring to any partnerships.

Activity:

Spend time with family and friends today, or having an outing by yourself. You've been pretty secluded for quite some time now. Slowly integrate yourself back into society.

Journal Entry:

If your money were more than plentiful, what causes would you contribute to and why? What are some other ways you can contribute your time, energy, and resources to these causes?

Day 29

29 (twenty-nine)

Competence, alternative perspectives, humility, and altruism

Affirmation of the Day:

I Am inspired to put action behind my goals every single day.

Theme Song:

"Finish Strong" by Naomi Raine

The only thing that is constant in and of this Universe is change. Everything and everybody changes. Which direction we decide to flow is left up to our own free will. In order to invite forward-motion transformation, we must first heal what's been holding us hostage for so long.

New opportunities are sometimes right in our face. We either don't recognize them or we feel we aren't ready for them. When spiritual transformation comes knocking at your door, it's not asking you to invite it in, it's commanding you to. When you shut the door on the opportunity presented to evolve, you only send yourself back through past cycles of hard lessons to learn — or in this case, re-learn.

Maybe you've been feeling stuck lately. Or maybe at every turn in your life there seems to be a conflict that arises and raw emotions begin to spill out. These are tell-tale signs that you are on the brink of a major shift in your life.

Does your relationship/marriage leave you feeling unsatisfied? Is your job unfulfilling? Are you having a difficult time communicating with your children? These types of moments and feelings often cause us to blame and judge others because we don't want to take responsibility and accountability for the role we play in our own discontent. We also sometimes develop a fear of losing what we've worked so hard to build, even though it is no longer what we want.

Change and transformation is natural. Trust the process. If you are getting big signs from the Universe, pay attention and flow accordingly. You're being offered the answers and support you need in this moment to get you to where you ultimately desire to be. You get tested the most when it's time for you to elevate. Don't break.

In what ways or areas do you wish you were more courageous? Now, imagine yourself as a bold and fearless master manifestor. What difference could you make by taking on these attributes?

Day 30

30 (thirty)

Supreme creativity, social certainty, honesty, openness, fun, inspiration, and imagination

Affirmation of the Day:

I Am proud of who I Am becoming.

Theme Song:

"Girl On Fire" by Alicia Keys

It's celebration time! Yes, you did it! The number 30 comes to parlay with you too. In dealing with the number 3 before, we know it denotes a time for all things fun. It invites our inner child to come out and play. Unleash your creativity to the world. Self-express your most authentic truth through whatever artistic medium your soul desires.

The 0's essence encourages wholeness and inclusiveness. The number 0 is nothing and everything at the same time. It represents the circle of life, implying every ending having a new beginning, and it all comes back around full circle. With that being said, revisit and repeat this 30-day cycle as many times as you need to. I have taken 30 days to unplug and self-care every year since 2020.

Remember — you are boundless with immeasurable potential. You are a manifesting beast. Continue to listen to your inner divine guidance, especially when making important decisions. Trust that you are always guided, protected, and provided for.

As you merge back into the world, be sure to keep a good balance between your career, home life, and time for yourself. Be mindful not to overdo it to a point of exhaustion. You've worked entirely too hard to pedal backwards.

Only intend to show up in ways that align with your truest self. The people that are supposed to be in this next level of your life will effortlessly feel drawn to you. Accept them with no guards up. Allow yourself to be free, transparent, and collaborative. Walk gracefully in your divine femininity. Receive all the blessings this life has for you.

Transform your 30 Days of Me, to 30 Days of We.

Journal Entry:

What are your three biggest takeaways from this 30-day journey?

La Ammitai

In a climate where personal development and entrepreneurship is now becoming "The American Dream", La Ammitai is committed to help guide others to their passions, purpose, and fulfill their most grand desires. She is a highly sought out Transformation Strategist, Master Numerologist, and a #1 Best Selling Author.

In all her work, La utilizes numerology as the catalyst to leverage personal and professional success for her clients. She also specializes in: NLP practices, inner child healing, law of attraction, and manifestation. La has transformed many lives with her unique approach to self-awareness. Her transparent, action-prone approach soars her clients to the best version of themselves.

La is a contributing author to bestselling books, *Power House Voices: Amazing Experiences on Clubhouse* and *The Marketing Stuff: Presenting Your Book to the World* — with many more books to come.

www.authorlaammitai.com